B–24J, 98th Bomb Group, 15th Air Force, Italy. In Desert pink and pale blue scheme.

# CONSOLIDATED B-24D-M LIBERATOR
## IN USAAF·RAF·RAAF·MLD·IAF·CzechAF & CNAF SERVICE
## PB4Y-1/2 PRIVATEER IN USN·USMC·AERONAVALE & CNAF SERVICE

**Illustrated & compiled by**
**Richard Ward**

**Text by**
**Ernest R. McDowell**

ACKNOWLEDGEMENTS

This book on the Liberator is the first title in the AIRCAM AVIATION SERIES to deal with a multi-engined bomber and is the first of two books covering the Liberator and Privateer during their long period of service during the wartime and postwar years. Volume 2 is in course of preparation now and will not duplicate in any way the content of this book. Many thanks to all those who assisted with photographs and information, without whose help the publication of this book would not have been possible. My thanks to all whose names are listed below in alphabetical order;

Peter M. Bowers, P. Boer, Richard M. Bueschel, Jean Cuny, J. E. H. Fail, R. C. Jones, G. H. Kamphuis, Dave Lucabaugh, Ernest R. McDowell, E. Munday, Merle T. Olmstead, Earl Reinert, Frank F. Smith, –. Stacey, Stan Staples, Zdenek Titz, United States Air Force, United States Marine Corps, Imperial War Museum, Australian War Museum, Establishment Cinematographique des Armees (ECA).

PB4Y–1 Privateer, VMD 154, 1st Marine Air Wing, USMC, South Pacific. Note fixed 20 mm cannon, offset to port so as not to obstruct the bomb-sight panel. Army OD and grey scheme, legend on fin in yellow reads: NAVY PB4Y–1 31946. Flown by the CO., Lt.Col. Elliot E. Bard.

PUBLISHED BY
Arco Publishing Company, Inc., 219 Park Avenue South, New York, N.Y. 10003
First Published by Osprey Publications Ltd. and Printed in Great Britain
Library of Congress No. 74-93933 · Library Edition SBN 668-02116-0 · Paperback Edition SBN 668-02115-2

B-24J's of the 464th Bomb Group, 15th Air Force, release their bombs on the rail yards at Heiligenstadt, Vienna, Austria, March 22nd 1945. (USAF).

# CONSOLIDATED PB4Y-1/2 PRIVATEER

1
PB4Y-1, unit unknown. US Navy, Standard USN Sea-search scheme, UK based.

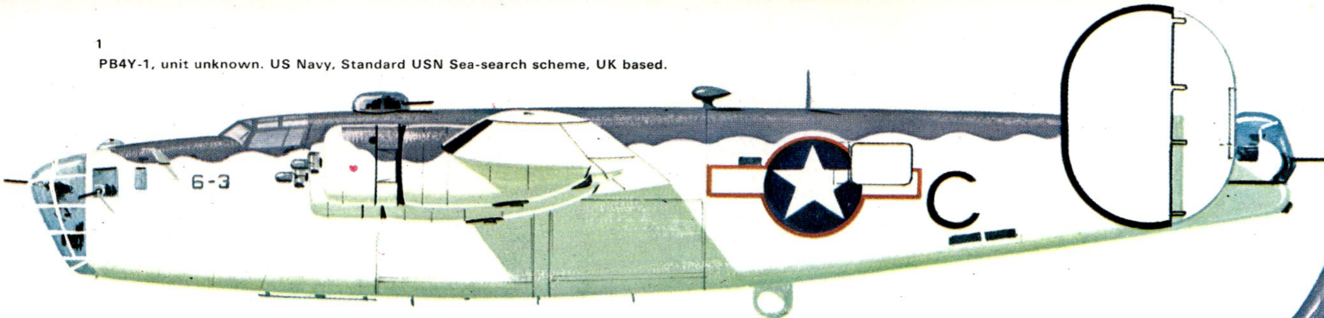


2
PB4Y-2, unit unknown. US Navy. Sea blue/grey and white scheme. 'Our Baby'.

3
PB4Y-1, Naval Aircraft Modification Unit, Johnsville, PA. US Navy.

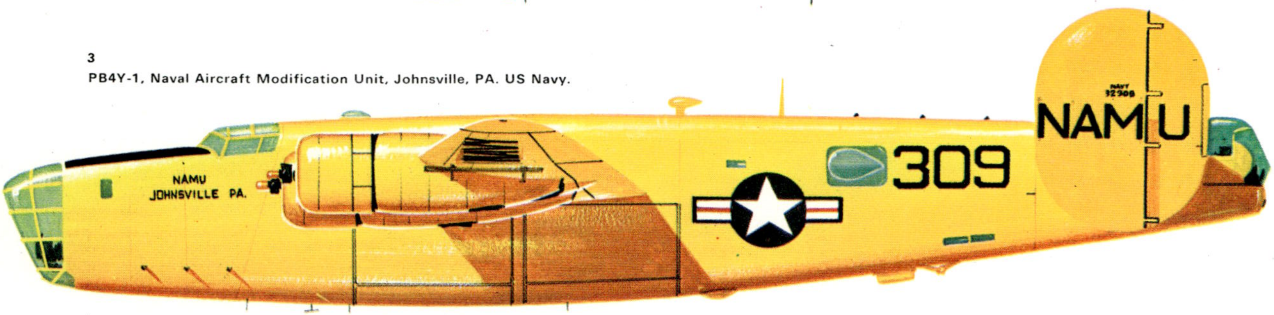


4
PB4Y-2, Escadrille 8F (subsequently 28F), Aeronavale.

15th Air Force Liberators of the 461st Bomb Group weave vapour trails high over Austria. (USAF).

# CONSOLIDATED B-24 LIBERATOR

The Consolidated model 32, designated the B-24 by the USAAF, was bound to achieve a certain amount of success based on sheer numbers alone. It was produced in greater numbers and in more versions than any other American airplane during World War II. A grand total of 18,188 were built if one takes into account all of the variants. They rolled off the Convair production lines at San Diego, California, and Fort Worth, Texas. Others were built by Ford Motors at Willow Run, Michigan, by Douglas Aircraft at Tulsa, Oklahoma, and finally by North American at Dallas, Texas.

The first production Liberators went to the British as LB-30As and were pretty much the same aircraft as the YB-24s. Liberator Is equipped 120 Squadron of the RAF's Coastal Command. The B-24A joined the USAAF at about this time which was early in June of 1941. Later the US Navy took delivery of a large number of Liberators which they designated the PB4Y-1. Liberators were pressed into service with the RAAF and the SAAF as well as the RAF. The various marks of the Liberator from I through VIII were used by at least 41 RAF squadrons at one time or another. The RAAF had four squadrons of Liberators in action. Forty-six USAAF groups flew the B-24 in combat. Others utilized it in training of aircrews and various other activities.

Cargo versions were designated as the C87 and C109 by the USAAF and as the C.VI and C.VIII by the British. The photo version was designated the F-7 by the Air Force and the PB4Y-1P by the Navy. A bomber escort version was modified as the XB-41 but never got into combat.

Besides its use as a strategic bomber it also served as a maritime reconnaissance aircraft, for anti-submarine operations, as a passenger transport, as a freighter, for photo recon, as a flying tanker, and in any number of other roles.

Comparing it to the B-17 has always been a favorite past time and on pure statistics alone it would appear to have all the better of the argument. It was faster, could carry a heavier bomb load, and could carry it higher and farther than the Fort. It was slightly more maneuverable and was much more adaptable to other tasks.

On the minus side, however, it was harder to fly, less stable, and very difficult to hold in the tight formations that were mandatory in the ETO. It also simply could not absorb the battle damage and remain in the air that the Fort was noted for and hence was not as popular with the air crews. Any sort of a solid hit on a wing meant almost certain death or at best capture for the crew as the Davis wing simply folded up when hit. It was a great innovation from the standpoint of aerodynamic efficiency but was a dead loss so far as battle damage was concerned and the twin fin and rudder did not stand up much better when hit either. This accounts for the lack of photos of B-24's to match the ones showing B-17's with great chunks of wings shot away, with half of the tail shot away or with great gaps in the fuselage. There were a few Libs that did take a lot of lead and make it back but few had vital hits on them.

As previously mentioned the B-24 was not exactly the airplane new crews dreamed of being assigned to, but once they were given the bird they made the most of it and earned their share of glory and medals. Liberator crews won their fair share of Congressional Medals of Honor.

The Liberator spawned almost as many different nicknames as it did variants. Most were decidedly uncomplimentary and while they didn't always get service wide

LB-30, one of 15 repossessed from a British (ex-French) contract. Four of these LB-30's saw operational service with the 7th Bomb Group in Java, three aircraft of this Group made the first operational mission of the Liberator during the War flown by USAAF crews, on January 16th 1942 operating from Singosari Field, Malang. (Peter M. Bowers).

recognition they were pretty well known to any one connected with bombers. Among the more common and better known ones were flying bath tub, flying coffin, flying boxcar, and the aerial street car. Lesser known ones were really gems. Among these were the combat crew Liquidator, the Constipated Libertine, the Convulsive Leviathian, the Compulsive Lumberer, and one or two names that cannot be mentioned in polite society.

The B-24 made its maiden flight on December 29th, 1939, as the XB-24. The company then received an order for seven test YB-24s and an evaluation set of 36 B-24s. Although the XB-24 weighed 41,000 lbs., the YB-24 grossed out at 46,400 lbs. and the weight kept going up as the B-24A had a maximum all up weight of 53,000 lbs. The top gross of 56,000 was reached in the H model.

The Liberator probably was fitted with more different gun turrets than any other bomber, Martin upper, Sperry ball, Consolidated, Boulton-Paul tail and Emerson nose turrets were all used at one time or another plus hand held mounts and chin turrets.

### Combat Operations with the USAAF

The 5th Air Force in the South West Pacific area had a total of four groups assigned, these were the 22nd, 43rd, 90th, and 380th groups. The 22nd traded its B-25s and B-26s for Liberators in February of 1944 and operated them until the war ended. The 43rd had switched from Forts to B-24s in an extended period covering May through September of '43. The other two groups, the 90th and 380th, were Liberator groups from their beginning.

The 22nd concentrated mainly on bombing, only flying a few armed recon missions over southern Japan very late in the war. Targets were airfields, shipping, and oil fields in Ceram, Halmahera and Borneo areas. The Southern Philippines began receiving attention in September of 44 as the 22nd hit key Japanese targets to pave the way for the Leyte landings and then switched to targets on Luzon. Later they flew close support to the Australians on Borneo and raided industrial and rail targets on Formosa and in China.

The 43rd after getting its B-24s while at Port Moresby experimented with skip bombing and employed these tactics against Japanese ships during the Battle of the Bismarck Sea. This mission brought the group a DUC. They continued to operate against enemy shipping in the Bismarck Archipelago and off the Dutch East Indies. They also took out airfields and Jap bases on New Guinea, Yap, Palau, the Celebes, Halmahera and the Southern Philippines, plus a few extra long range raids against Ceram and Borneo.

On June 16th, 1943, a B-24 took off on a long range photo-recon mission alone to photograph vital targets in the Solomons. The mission produced two Congressional Medals of Honor. A crew of misfits skippered by Capt. Jay Zeamer had volunteered for the mission knowing fully well it would be a rough one. At the missions end Capt. Zeamer and his Bombardier, Lt. Joseph R. Sarnoski, had earned Congressional Medals of Honor. After getting the photos the Liberator was jumped by a force of about twenty Jap Zeros who made pass after pass at them. Capt. Zeamer was wounded, so was Lt. Sarnoski, but both continued to fight on. Lt. Sarnoski kept firing the nose guns until he died and Zeamer fought to keep the bomber in the air and to get the rest of the crew home alive. Somehow or other they managed to limp home across 500 miles of ocean and make a safe landing.

The group was moved first to the Philippines and then to Ie Shima and from the latter raided airfields, railroad yards and shipping in the Inland Sea and the Sea of Japan.

The 90th was hurriedly moved to Hawaii in September of 1941 and assigned to the 7th Air Force while it completed its training. In November 42 they moved on to Australia to join the 5th Air Force and went into action at once. For the most part the 90th's missions were similar to those of the 22nd. They even participated in the same battles. Their DUC was won for raids on Wewak in September 1943 when they flew through heavy flak and fighter patrols.

The 380th, though a member of the 5th Air Force, was attached to the RAAF until January 1945 and along with regular duties engaged in the training of RAAF combat crews. They entered combat in May of 43. The group was awarded a DUC for long range raids on Balikpapan, Borneo, in August and later picked up a second DUC while supporting the American landing at Hollandia. The 380th flew the same type missions as the others with one exception—after the war ended they ferried prisoners of

LB-30 showing clearly the U.S. Flag on the nose and U.S. ARMY under the wings. The RAF serial is still faintly discernable on the fuselage ahead of the tailplane. This particular Liberator flew Mr. W. A. Harriman on a supply and fact finding mission to Singapore shortly before the Japanese attack. (IWM).

war from Japan to Manila.

In the Central Pacific area the 7th Air Force held sway with its four B-24 groups. These included the 11th, 30th, 307th, and 494th. The 11th began its career with the 7th was reassigned to the 13th and then returned to the 7th again in March of 43. Rejoining the 13th meant re-equipping with B-24s and after a training period they returned to combat operations in November. Operating out of Funafuti they took part in the Marshalls, Gilberts, and Marianas operations before moving to Guam in October 1944. From Guam they raided the Volcano and Bonin Islands, concentrating on air fields, shipping, and installations. The 11th was on Okinawa when the wars end came but they continued to fly armed recon and survelliance missions to China and to ferry POW's from Okinawa to Luzon.

The 30th went into combat from the Ellice Islands during November of 1943. They supported the invasions of the Gilberts, Tarawa, and the Marshalls by hitting air fields in these areas. Moving to Kwajalein in March of 44 they raided Truk to keep it neutralized while the attack on Marianas was mounted. They also hit Guam, Saipan, and Wake and in 1944 found themselves moving to Saipan which had fallen to the Allies. From their new base they pasted the Bonin and Volcano Islands in support of the forces invading Iwo Jima. They continued to hit by-passed areas in the Carolinas and Marianas until they finally were ordered back to Hawaii in 1945.

The 307th began operations by flying search and patrol missions from Hawaii. In December of 42 and January of 43 they staged through Midway Island to bomb Wake Island. Later they moved to Guadalcanal when it was secured and became a part of the 13th Air Force.

The 494th moved to Palau in September of 1944 but before being able to go on operations they had to aid in the construction of their own base. When the base on Angaur was finished they began their raids on Yap and Korar and also hit by-passed islands. Later the Philippines came in for a major share of their operations. Hitting various targets on Corregidor and Caballo they moved up the islands, Clark Field became a prime target and early in 1945 they began hitting air bases in Mindanao, supply depots on the Davao Gulf and Illana Bay Area. Moving up to Okinawa they started a campaign against air fields on Kyushu which were ended by V-J Day. Among their missions they had dropped propaganda leaflets, incendiaries, and finally wound up transporting personnel and materials from Manila to Tokyo after the war ended.

The Southwest Pacific area was the stamping grounds of the 13th Air Force and its two groups, the 5th and 307th. The 5th was an old organization that dated back to 15 August, 1919, when it was formed in Hawaii. The group's motto "Kaai Oka Lewa" is Hawaiian meaning "The Guardians of the Upper Regions". Leaving the Island of Hawaii in November of 1942 they joined the 13th at Espiritu Santo arriving there on December 1st. Many long photo recon missions were scheduled for the group in the Solomons and over the Coral Sea. In turn raids were laid on to Bougainville, New Britain, New Ireland and finally to Woleai where they won a DUC for action over this bitterly defended island. New targets were assigned with Yap, Truk, and the Palaus being bombed to pave the way for the Leyte operation. A second DUC came their way from a raid on the Balikpapan oil refineries on September 30, 1944. They then went on to fly numerous missions in the Philippines till the war ended.

The 307th joined the 13th Air Force on Guadalcanal and operated in the same areas that the 5th Group did. They won a DUC for an unescorted daylight attack on Truk on March 29, 1944. Their second DUC was won on a raid to Balikpapan which had to be one of the toughest targets in the area to hit early in the war. Finally they parted company with the targets that the 5th was hitting and were sent to support the Australian troops on Borneo and then bombed targets in Indo-China during the three final months of the war. They ferried POWs from Okinawa to Manila.

B-34J in overall glossy black finish. Serial 250682.

XB-24Q with radar tail turret. Serial 449916.

B-24H with remote control side turrets. Serial 27127.

B-24M Modified with tail gun radar. Serial 451922.

Above: B-24M Modified. Serial 451922.

Below: Early C-87. Serial 439229 (photos P. M. Bowers).

B-24D 'Hellsadroppin II' of the 93rd Bomb Group, 8th Air Force, ETO. See colour illustration. (USAF).

**European Operations**

The 8th Air Force operated at least twenty groups that were equipped with B-24's at one period or another during their operational life. It obviously will be impossible to list the achievements of each group in so limited a text as this, however, it will be possible to list some of the highlights of these groups. Included in the list are the 34th, 44th, 93rd, 389th, 392nd, 445th, 446th, 448th, 453rd, 458th, 466th, 467th, 482nd, 486th, 487th, 489th, 490th, 491st, 492nd, and 493rd.

The 2nd Air Division consisted of four B-24 wings each consisting of three groups. This was the one that used Liberators during most of the war. Liberator groups hit all of the well known targets in occupied Europe and Nazi Germany as well as many lesser known sites.

The 44th operating from Shipham, England, won two DUC's and its CO, Col. Leon Johnson, was awarded the CMH for leading his squadron in the attack on the Ploesti Oil Fields that produced their second DUC. The first had been received for hitting Naval targets at Kiel. The 93rd's record closely paralled the 44ths. They won DUCs, one while on detached service in North Africa for operating under extremely difficult conditions against enemy shipping and supply depots. The second like that of the 44th came in the Ploesti raid; they received two CMHs when Lt.-Col. Addison E. Baker and Major John L. Jerstad refused to ditch a seriously damaged B-24 went on in to hit the target and then went down in the target area. The awards were posthumous.

The 389th also received a DUC for the Ploesti attack and 2nd Lt. Lloyd H. Hughes received the CMH when he bored on in to hit the target though his flak damaged aircraft was losing gasoline and crashed while attempting a belly landing after completing the bomb run in the target area. The 392nd received a DUC while operating from Wendling, England, during Big Week when they blasted the Gotha factory complex. The 445th was awarded the Croix de Guerre with Palm by the French for their part in the theater from December 43 to February 45. They also received a DUC for a raid on Gotha.

The 489th produced another Congressional Medal winner in Lt.-Col. Leon R. Vance, whose Liberator was hit by flak while bombing coastal defenses on June 5th, 1944. His right foot was almost severed by flak while leading the formation, his pilot was killed and Vance took the controls, led the group in to a successful bombing run, flew back to England. He ordered the crew to bail out but remained with the ship because he thought that one of the crew was unable to bail out. He then ditched in the Channel and was rescued. The 491st won its DUC when after being intercepted by enemy fighters and losing half of their planes they still fought through and successfully bombed the target.

The 492nd had a rather unique job and name, "The Carpetbaggers", which covered clandestine operations assigned to the group. They dropped secret agents, supplies, and equipment to the underground. They also dropped leaflets and other propaganda material. A halt was called and they trained and became a night bomber outfit to hit targets in Germany, then it was back to Carpetbagging again, this time operating over Germany rather than France. They received a DUC and a citation from the French for these activities which at times were carried out not only in darkness but many times in poor weather as well. The original group had been withdrawn from combat after suffering excessive losses losing 53 aircraft in combat in less than three months not counting accidents.

**North Africa and Mediterranean Theater**

Besides these various groups of the 8th mentioned above that were detached for various brief periods and sent to North Africa three Air Forces operated in the area, these were the 9th, which later was transferred to England, the 12th, and the 15th. The 9th had two groups attached to it, the 98th and 376th. The 98th won two DUCs as a group and had two CMH's presented to individuals. The 376th was one of the few groups to win three DUCs.

The 98th began operations with the 9th, was transferred to the 12th when the 9th went to England and finally was reassigned to the 15th late in the war. The group was awarded its first DUC for action in the Middle East, North Africa, and Sicily from August 42 until August 43. Its second came at Ploesti as did both of its Medals of Honor. The Group CO, Col. John R. Kane, received one of the Medals for leading the group while the other was won by 1st Lt. Donald D. Pucket. Lt. Pucket's B-24 was hit and the crew members started to panic as several were wounded. He calmed them, gave first aid, checked the damage and realizing that they would not be able to make it back he gave the order to bail out. He elected to stay with the ship because three crew members were too badly hurt to jump. A few moments later unable to gain sufficient altitude or turn the damaged plane quickly enough it hit a mountainside and exploded killing all aboard.

The 376th, known as the Liberandos, received their first DUC for the action in the Middle East, North Africa, and Sicily the same as the 98th did. The second came when they attempted to hit Ploesti after getting off course and approaching from the wrong direction in the big raid. The defense had been fully alerted and the 376th was clobbered badly. Their third DUC was awarded for a raid on the oil industries around Bratislava on June 16, 1944. Not only was this group one of the very few to win three DUCs but it also probably was the only one to win them while flying with three different Air Forces, getting one each with the 9th, 12th and 15th.

B-24H, 44th Bomb Group, 8th Air Force, dropping its load on Frankfurt, 29th January 1944. Serial 27644. (IWM).

The groups assigned to the 12th were covered above so will be passed over here. The 15th Air Force had a total of 15 groups attached to it at one time or another. These included the 98th, 376th, 449th, 450th, 451st, 454th, 455th, 456th, 460th, 461st, 465th, 484th, and the 485th.

The 449th was awarded a pair of DUCs. The first for an unescorted mission to the marshalling yards at Bucharest. Attacked by a large number of enemy fighters they fought their way to the target, hit it, and fought their way out destroying a number of enemy fighters in the process. Their second DUC was won, as so many were, for a raid on Ploesti on July 9, 1944. The 450th received a DUC for carrying out a raid on the Messerschmidt plant at Regensburg under almost impossible weather conditions when the others had turned back. Their second came when they fought their way in and out to hit the marshalling yards—at Ploesti! The 451st got three DUCs, for raids on Regensburg, an aerodrome at Vienna, and the Ploesti marshalling yards.

The 454th won its two DUCs without having to visit Ploesti to get them. They were awarded for raids on the aerodrome at Bad Voslau and a steel plant at Linz. Two highly successful missions that virtually wiped out a ball bearing plant at Steyr and an oil refinery at Moosbeirbaum brought a pair of DUCs to the 455th. The fact that two other groups turned back failed to deter the 456th from pressing on to their target at Wiener-Neustadt and scoring numerous direct hits. Their determination brought them their first DUC. A second one was earned for a well planned and executed raid on the oil refinery complex at Budapest. Lead missions through intense flak and in the face of enemy fighters brought DUCs to the 459th who led the 304th wing to Bad Voslau and to the 460th for leading the raid on Zwolfaxing. Two DUCs went to the 461st for a raid on Budapest and another one to the glory target—Ploesti! The 464th led the 55th Wing to Vienna gaining a DUC in the process and then picked up number two when they hit the oil refinery at Pardubice a crippling blow. The 465th matched these two by getting a pair for hitting Vienna and Fredrichshafen despite an all out attempt to prevent them from getting through by the Nazis.

While these recitations of awards of the Distinguished Unit Citation may tend to become a bit boring it must be remembered that such awards were made only for extraordinary efforts and not run of the mill milk runs. They were given for superbly planned and carried out missions, for missions pressed home in spite of tremendous odds and at great cost in lives due to losses, and in all cases for courage and devotion to duty. They were never given, they were always won! That so many B-24 groups earned them speaks very well for the Liberator. That so many crew members won the Congressional Medal of Honor speaks volumes for the courage of these men.

### Other Theaters of Operations

The North Pacific area has generally been overlooked as the aerial operations were relatively light and unspectacular as well as limited by conditions. Despite this the 28th Group, the lone B-24 outfit in the 11th Air Force, managed to bring home a DUC near the end of the war for operations against the Kuril Islands late in 1945. These missions called for long flights over the Arctic wastes in the worst sort of weather and they forced the Japanese to pull out a few fighters and send them to defend this area.

In Asia a single Liberator group operated as a part of the 14th Air Force. The 308th won two DUCs. The first for an unescorted bombing attack on the docks and other installations at Hankow, and the second for a series of interdiction raids against Japanese shipping during 1944-45.

The Groups Commanding Officer, Maj. Horace S. Carswell, was awarded the Medal of Honor when he elected to remain with a badly damaged B-24 because his bombardier's chute had been ripped to shreds by flak. The co-pilot also elected to stay and try to help Carswell bring the ship in for an emergency landing. The bombardier apparently did not feel that he could accept one of their chutes so he too remained and all three were killed when the plane hit a mountainside and burned. Shortly before this Major Carswell, flying with another crew, had come upon a Japanese convoy and they had damaged a destroyer when they sighted a cruiser. The bombardier, a member of Class 43-13 from the Advanced Bombardier School at Midland, Texas, one of the outstanding classes of the war, Lt. Nolan "Snuffy" Klepinger, put a stick of bombs directly on the cruiser, one went right into the magazine and the ship blew up and sank within a matter of minutes. Klepinger received the DSC for his accuracy.

Left: Nice plan view shot of a Liberator of the 467th Bomb Group, 8th Air Force, showing Group letter on black disc on starboard wing. Target: rail yards Osnabrook, 23rd March 1945. (USAF).
Right: B-24H of the 389th Bomb Group during attack on St. Malo, France. (USAF).

In the CBI the 10th Air Force also was limited to a single B-24 Group. The 7th was another of the pre-war groups that dated back to 1919. This was the group that was en route to the Philippines when the Japs hit Pearl Harbor and a flight of six of their B-17's arrived during the attack and managed to get in safely. After being sent to Java and losing most of their airplanes in the bitter fighting early in the war the 7th was sent to India in 1942 and assigned to the 10th. It went into combat with a mixture of B-17s and LB-30s, finally converting to all B-24s late in '42. Hitting just about any kind of a target imaginable in Burma, Thialand, China, and on the Andaman Sea, they built up a good record quickly. A DUC was forthcoming for a raid staged on March 19, 1945, on rail lines and bridges in Thialand. Another phase in their career was transporting aviation gasoline over the Hump into China.

The 6th Air Force in the Canal Zone had two groups of B-24s based in Panama, these were the 6th and 9th, and both were senior groups. The 6th dated from 1919 and the 9th from 1922. Both had been formed in the Canal Zone, both flew protective patrols and anti-submarine sea searches. The 6th was disbanded on November 1, 1943, while the 9th was sent back to the States where it was used in training cadres for bomb groups and to test new equipment with a mixed complement of B-24s, B-17s and B-26s.

In the Zone of the Interior three of the four numbered Air Forces, the 1st, 2nd, and 4th all had B-24 groups attached. The First had the 400th and 471st. The Third had none assigned. The 4th had the 399th and the 470th but the big Liberator Air Force in the States was the Second with no fewer than 10 groups attached. These were the 302nd, 304th, 331st, 346th, 383rd, 399th, 400th, 470th, and 471st. The Second took over all B-24 groups eventually. All of these groups were engaged in training operations. Their main duties were to either turn out complete combat crews ready to operate as a team or to ready individual replacements for overseas groups to fill in crews that had lost members in combat. Other B-24s found their ways in small lots to various other training schools later in the war. Thus a fledgling gunner or Cadet Bombardier might find himself firing from a turret or dropping bombs from the same type of aircraft he would be assigned to in actual combat. This speeded up training programs as the larger bomber could carry more students and bombs or ammo than the early small training planes like the AT-11. It saved fuel, cut down the number of take offs and landings, freed some of the pilots, instructors and other personnel needed previously to do the same job. Early in the war such planes could not be spared from the war zones for domestic training programs.

### The US Navy Liberators

Initially the USAAF operated B-24Ds on anti-submarine patrols, a duty that the Navy felt rightfully belonged to it. On July 7, 1942, an agreement was reached whereby the Navy would be allotted a number of the aircraft and as soon as they were ready to relieve the Air Force they would then phase out. The Navy designated the planes PB4Y-1s and by the end of the war had received a total of 977 of them. By August of 43 the Navy had begun to replace the B-24s with their PB4Y-1s. On May 3, 1943, CVAC also had been authorized to withdraw 3 B-24Ds from the production line and to convert them into the PB4Y-2 experimental prototypes. In time the Navy procured 739 of this type. The PB4Y-2 was given the name Privateer by the Navy but few got into action before the war ended. A large number continued in operation after the war and a transport type the RY-3 was also produced for the Navy. Forty-six of this version

Left: OD B24–H, 489th Bomb Group, 8th Air Force, note black W on white disc. Target: Shulan oil refinery, Hambourg. (USAF).

Right: B-24H of the 392nd Bomb Group, 8th Air Force, during attack on St. Dizier airfield, date unknown. Note black letter D on white disc, usual presentation on camouflaged aircraft. (USAF).

were built. The Privateer was extensively modified and hardly resembled the B-24s at all.

### Liberators in Allied Air Forces

Despite the fact that the major portion of this text is devoted to American employment of the B-24 no slight is intended so far as the Allied nations who also flew the aircraft are concerned. The very name Liberator was bestowed by the British and was used universally.

The RAF made extensive use of the Liberator. Obtaining over two thousand of these airplanes from Mark I through to Mark VIII the RAF had forty-one squadrons equipped with the plane and also a number of others flying small numbers of the Liberator as a part of their equipment. In the Mediterranean 37, 40, 70, 104, 148, 178, and 614 squadrons flew the bird. In the Far East it was operated by 99, 159, 160, 203, 215, 232, 233, 243, 246, 321, 354, 355, 356, 357, and 358 squadrons. In the United Kingdom 53, 59, 86, 102, 103, 120, 203, 214, 223, 224, 233, 246, 292, 301, 311, 422, 423, 426, 502, and 547 squadrons were Liberator equipped. In addition for a time 53 and 59 squadrons operated from Iceland and 206 and 220 squadrons operated from the Azores on convoy protective and anti-submarine duties. In the Far East the RAAF was represented by 21, 23, 24 and 25 squadrons. In the Mediterranean and Far East the RAF used its Liberators mainly on night bombing missions. Many Libs were assigned to the Coastal Command of the RAF and early in the war it was their long range performance that enabled the RAF to close the mid-Atlantic gap that had existed and provide a measure of air support for a convoy all the way across the Atlantic. Transport versions put in a very early appearance in British colors and were designated by a C in front of the mark number. One was even fitted as a personal plane for Sir Winston Churchill and named "Commando". The Liberator served the RAF long and well, many were still on hand when the Berlin Airlift came about in 1948 and saw much service in the lift. The RCAF and SAAF also received some Liberators and in the immediate post war period a large number found their way into the services of the South and Latin American air forces. Even today a few continue in service and some still are being used in civil aviation in Bolivia as transports. Even BOAC had a few in service right after the war. Today a few still are flying in South America. The Confederate Air Force has a Liberator in flying condition. The USAF Air Museum has one on display and another is in the National Air Museum's collection. Recently a group in San Diego have been attempting to collect enough money to ferry one back from India where it was just recently phased out by the Indian Air Force. A few converted to water carrying fire bombers still exist in the Pacific Northwest and Canada and a few others are rotting away in a few remote areas but the vast majority have long since vanished under the salvager's hammers and crucibles.

Above: B-24D, 93rd Bomb Group, 8th Air Force, in early markings, probably Nov./Oct. 1942. See colour illustration. (USAF).

Below: B-24D, 93rd Bomb Group, note red surround to the National Insignia and grey star and bar. Serial 272869. (USAF).

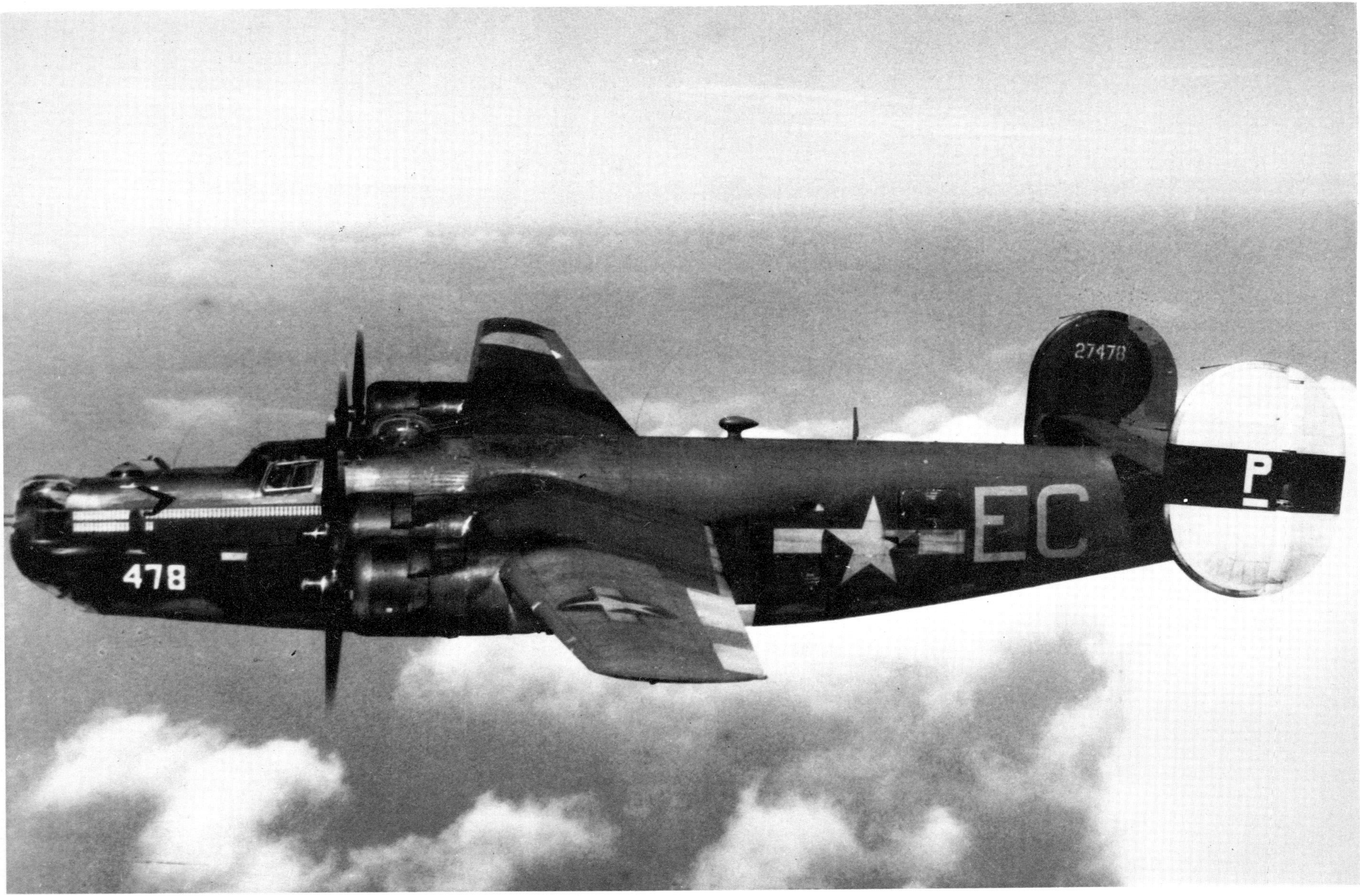

Very nice flying shot of a B-24H of the 44th Bomb Group, 8th Air Force, ETO. See colour illustration. (USAF).

Above: Liberators of the 458th Bomb Group, 8th Air Force, taxying out for take-off on the 200th mission, Horsham-St. Faith. 26th February 1945. (USAF).

Above: 'Final Approach' awaiting take-off for the 200th mission, serial 253457. (USAF).

Below: 'Gas House Mouse', a B-24H of the 458th Bomb Group, 8th Air Force, which made it back to Manston, Kent, emergency airfield. Note Lanc and Fort in background. Serial 295050. (USAF).

Above: 'The Shack' with added armour plate below cockpit revving up prior to take-off on the 200th mission, Horsham-St-Faith, 26th February 1945. (USAF).

Above: Formating ship of the 458th Bomb Group, 8th Air Force, ETO. See colour illustration. (USAF).

Above: 'Sharkmouthed' Formating Liberator of the 458th Bomb Group, this aircraft replaced the D after it was written off. (USAF via E. Munday).

Above: Close-up of the 'sharkmouth' on the 458th formating ship. (USAF).

Below: B-24H, 'Bi-U-Baby' taking off from an emergency strip near Lydd, Kent. 491st Bomb Group, Path Finder Force aircraft. Serial 295610. (USAF).

Above & below: With hydraulic systems shot out over Germany these two B-24H's of the 445th Bomb Group, 8th Air Force, land at their base with parachutes streaming in lieu of brakes. (photos USAF).

Below: B-24H of the 491st Bomb Group nosed over in soft ground at North Picham, August 1944. Green/white/green rudders, serial 295123. (via E. Munday).

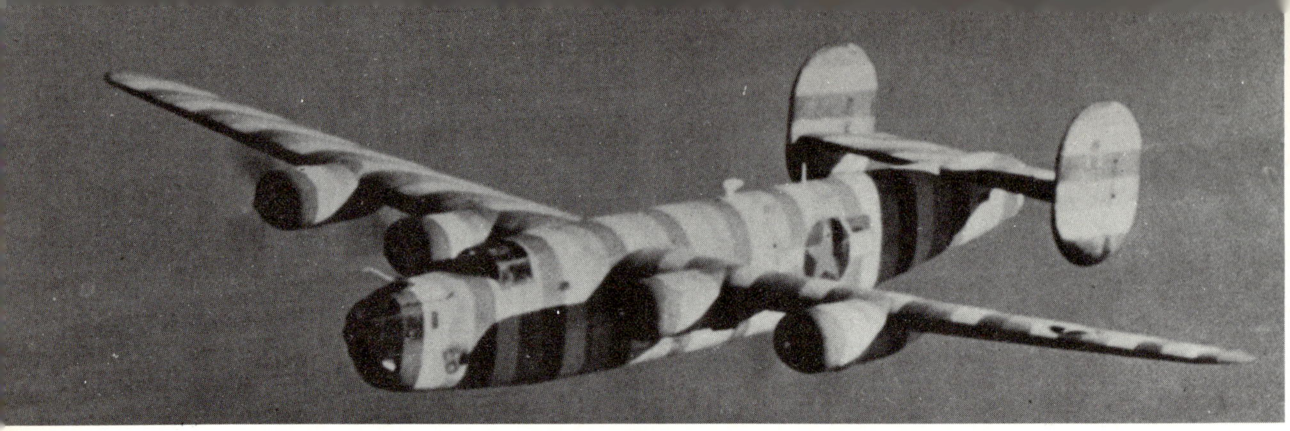

Above, two pictures: Formating aircraft of the 93rd Bomb Group, note rudder marking variations, colours unknown, serial probably 129537. (top USAF; above via E. Munday).

Left & below: Formating aircraft of the 466th Bomb Group, 8th Air Force, see colour illustration (left USAF, below Merle T. Olmstead).

Above: 44th Bomb Group formating ship, see colour illustration. (USAF).

Above: 445th Bomb Group formating aircraft, see colour illustration. (USAF).

Below: 491st Bomb Group during an attack on a German target. (USAF).

B-24D in desert sand camouflage of the 376th Bomb Group, 9th Air Force, coming in to land at Benghasi, Libya, after the attack on Ploesti, Rumania. (USAF)

Line-up of sand and OD camouflaged B-24D's of the 376th Bomb Group, Bengahsi, Libya. (USAF).

Above: A pair of B-34D's of the 376th Bomb Group. (IWM).

Left: 'Strawberry Bitch' a B-24D of the 376th Bomb Group, 'The Liberandos' 9th Air Force on a desert landing ground, probably Benghasi. This famous old aircraft is now preserved at the USAF Museum, Wright Patterson AFB. See colour illustration. (via E. R. McDowell).

Below: 'Chug-a-Lug' of the 98th Bomb Group, 15th Air Force, Italy, with 105 missions to her credit, 3 to Ploesti, is here shown returning from her last mission before returning to the States. (USAF)

Formation of B-24D's low over the Adriatic on their way to a target in Northern Italy. Unit unknown. (USAF).

B-24D of the 376th Bomb Group, 15th AF, flying past the snow covered cone of Mt. Vesuvius. (USAF).

Above: B-24D, 376th Bomb Group taxying down the waterlogged runway of its Italian base. (USAF).

Below: B-24D of the 484th Bomb Group, 15th AF, taking off from a Balkan airfield. (USAF).

Above: B-24M, 461st Bomb Group, 765th Squadron, 15th Air Force. (Stan Staples).

Above & below: White cowl rings denoted 765th Squadron, red horizontal bar on vertical tail surface 461st Bomb Group, red top half of fin/rudder 49th Bomb Wing. (Stan Staples).

Below: 765th Squadron taxying out for take-off on a bombing mission, 484th Bomb Group in distance. Torretto, Italy. (Stan Staples).

Above: B-24M of the 461st Bomb Group coming in on three engines. (Stan Staples).

Above: 'Billie K' the Radar 'Mickey' of the 461st Bomb Group, Cerignola, Italy. Flown back to the States by Stan Staples. (Stan Staples).

Below: Good detail shot of office area of 39. (Stan Staples).

Above: B-24J of the 451st Bomb Group, note flak damage to port wing. (IWM).

Above: B-24J, 451st Bomb Group, 15th Air Force, photo taken during attack on the Herman Goering Steel Works, Linz, Austria. (USAF).

Left: Damaged by flak over Ploesti this B-23J of the 451st Bomb Group belly lands at Castelluccio, Italy. (USAF).

Below: With one engine smoking a B-24J of the 451st Bomb Group flies through heavy flak over Vienna, Austria, 13th October 1944. (USAF).

Above: B-24M, 459th Bomb Group, 15th Air Force, in a bone-yard after the war.

Left: B–24J of the 449th Bomb Group, note white fuselage band aft of wings, parked near the water edge, Grottaglie, Italy, 5th October 1944. (USAF).

Below: Flak damaged B-24J of the 449th Bomb Group, Grottaglie, Italy. (F. F. Smith via E. Munday).

Above & below: B-24J's 304th Bomb Wing with hydraulics shot out used chutes as brakes to shorten landing roll. (photos USAF).

Above: A pair of B-24J's of the 450th Bomb Group leaving the target area, Theole-sur-Mer, near Cannes. Note white stripe round fuselage. (USAF).

Left: 'Buzz Job', a B-24J of the 485th Bomb Goup flying low over the Italian countryside. (Stacey).

Above: S, a B-24J of the 485th Bomb Group, taking off from Venosa, Italy. (Stacey).

Right: Q, an OD camouflaged B-24J of the 485th Bomb Group, 15th Air Force.

Left: B-24J of the 465th Bomb Group over the Appenines, Italy, 1945. (via E. Munday).

A

1

LB-30, one of 15 repossessed from a British (ex French) contract.

2

B-24J, 90th Bomb Group, 5th Air Force, SWPA.

3

B-24L, 11th Bomb Group, 431st Squadron, 7th Air Force, 'Bolivar Jr'.

4

B-24J, 11th Bomb Group, 7th Air Force.

5

B-24L, unit unknown, 14th Air Force, CBI.

6

B-24J, 308th Bomb Group, 375th Squadron, 14th Air Force, CBI.

1

B-24D, 93rd Bomb Group, 8th Air Force, ETO.

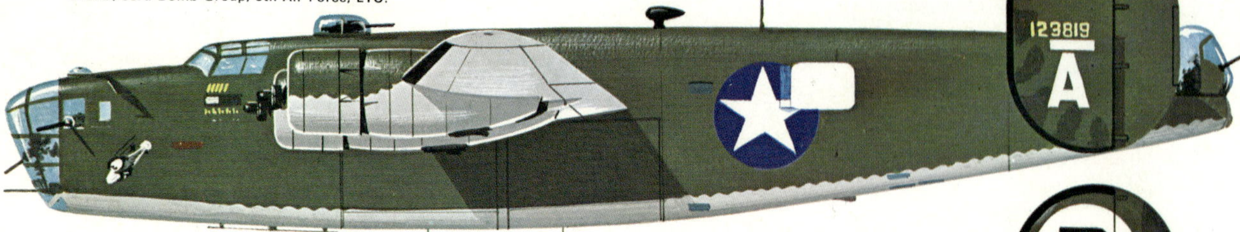


2

B-24D, 93rd Bomb Group, 8th Air Force, ETO. 'Hellsadroppin'.

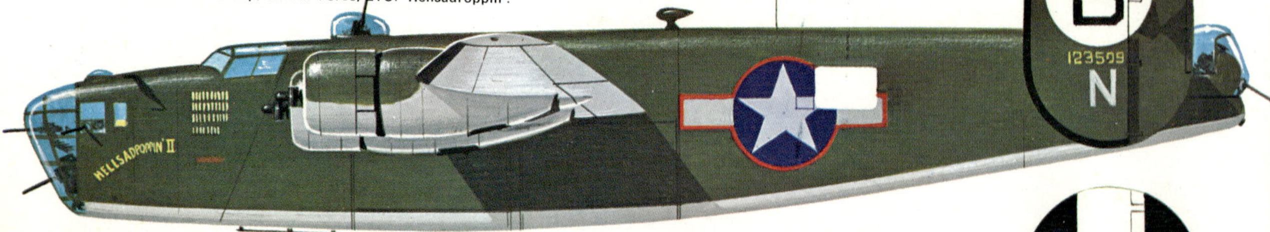


3

B-24J, 389th Bomb Group, 8th Air Force, ETO. 'The Sky Shark'.

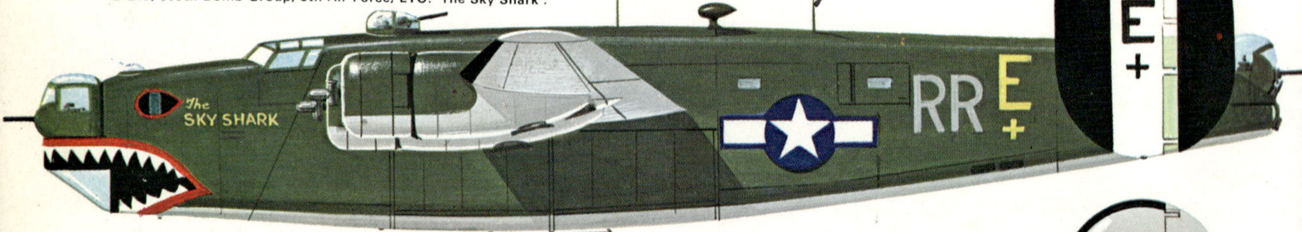


4

B-24H, 44th Bomb Group, 8th Air Force, ETO.

5

B-24D, Formating aircraft, 44th Bomb Group, 8th Air Force, ETO.

6

B-24J, 858th Bomb Squadron, Special Operations, 8th Air Force, ETO.

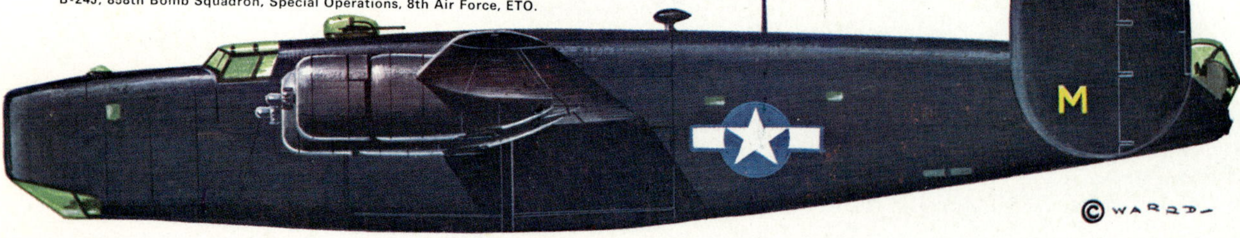

1
B-24D, Formating aircraft, 458th Bomb Group, 8th Air Force, ETO.

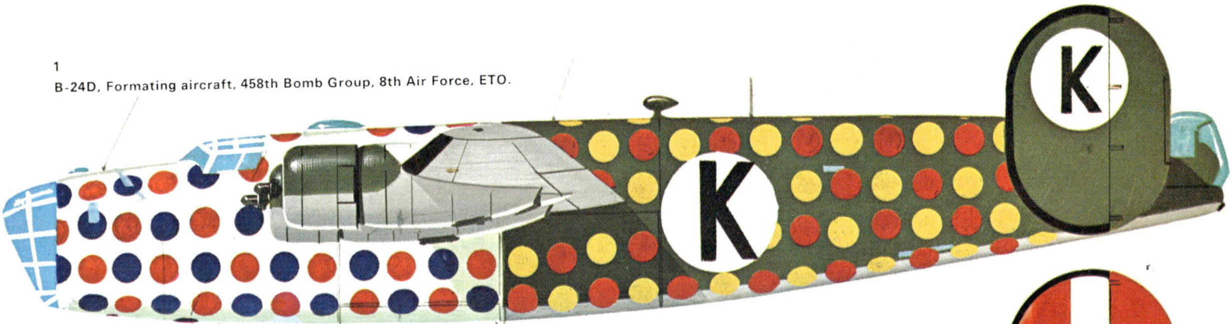


2
B-24J, Formating aircraft, 458th Bomb Group, 8th Air Force, ETO.

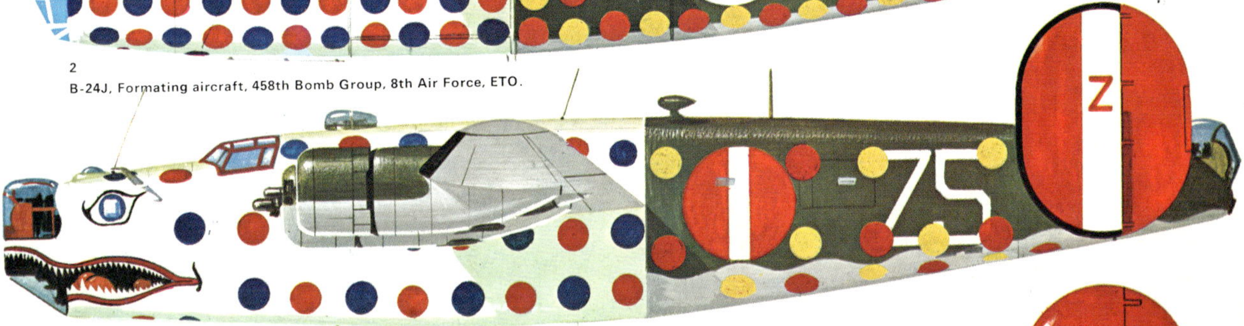


3
B-24D, Formating aircraft, 466th Bomb Group, 8th Air Force, ETO

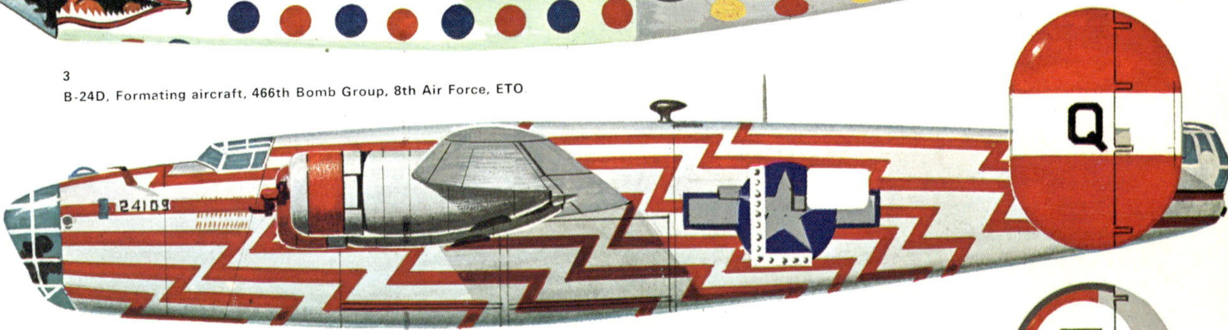


4
B-24D, Formating aircraft, 445th Bomb Group, 8th Air Force, ETO.

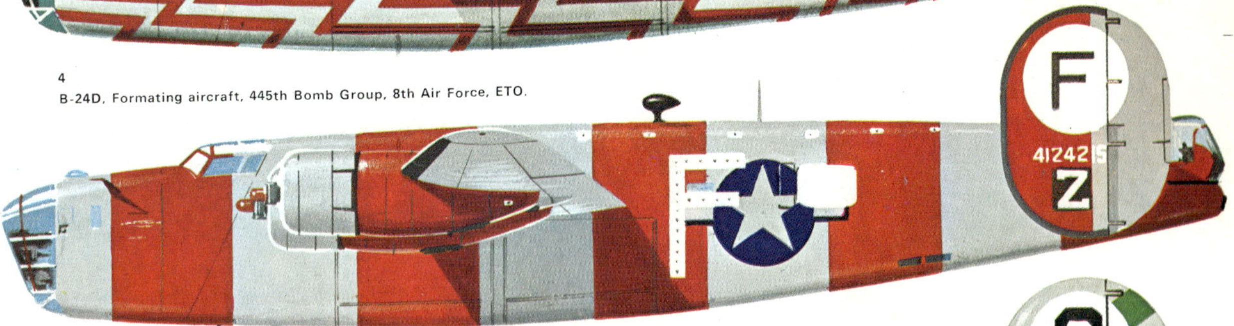


5
B-24D, Formating aircraft, 466th Bomb Group, 8th Air Force, ETO.

6
B-24J, Formating aircraft, 491st Bomb Group, 8th Air Force, ETO.

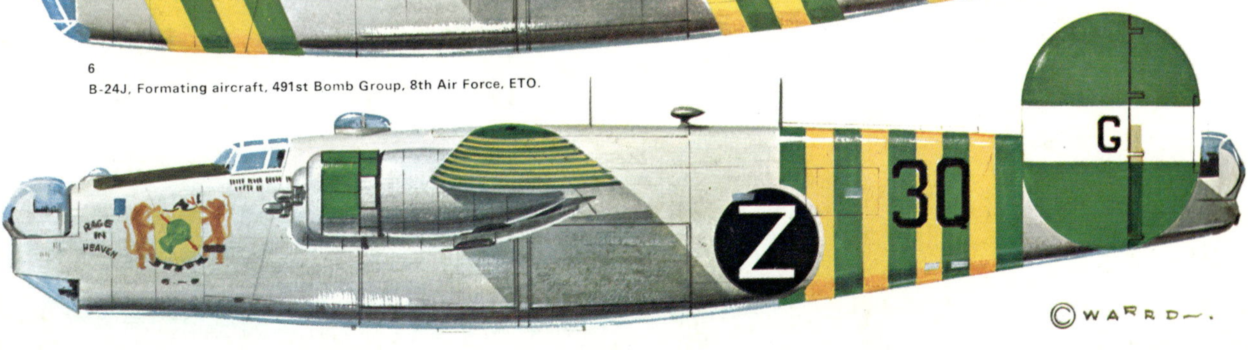

D

1

B-24M, 461st Bomb Group, 765th Squadron, 15th Air Force, Italy.

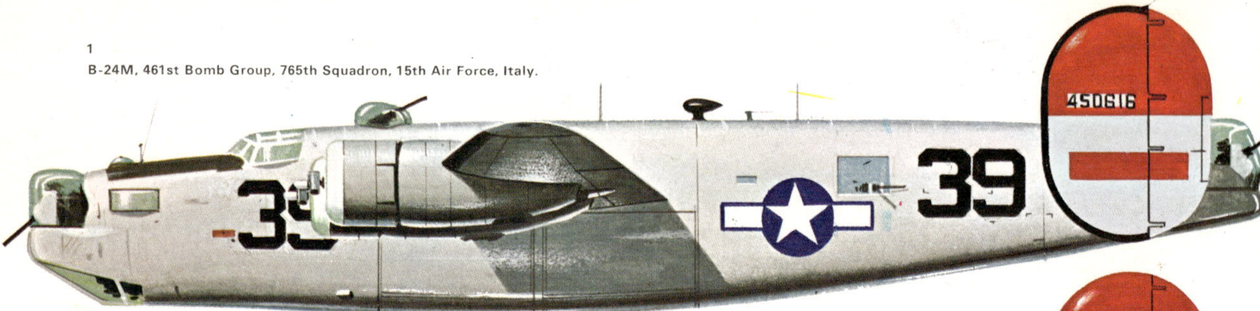


2

B-24M, Radar 'Mickey', 461st Bomb Group, 15th Air Force, Italy. 'Billie K'.

3

B-24J, 451st Bomb Group, 15th Air Force, Italy. 'Minnesota Mauler'.

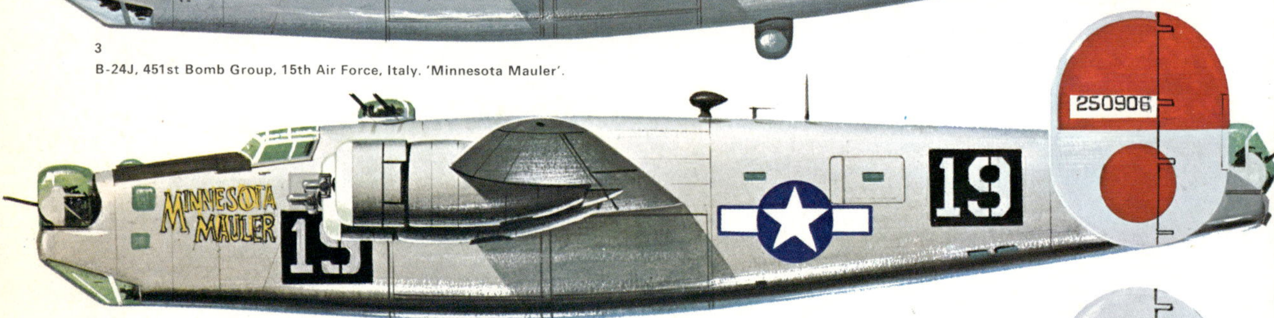


4

B-24J, 449th Bomb Group, 15th Air Force, Italy.

5

B-24J, 460th Bomb Group, 15th Air Force, Italy.

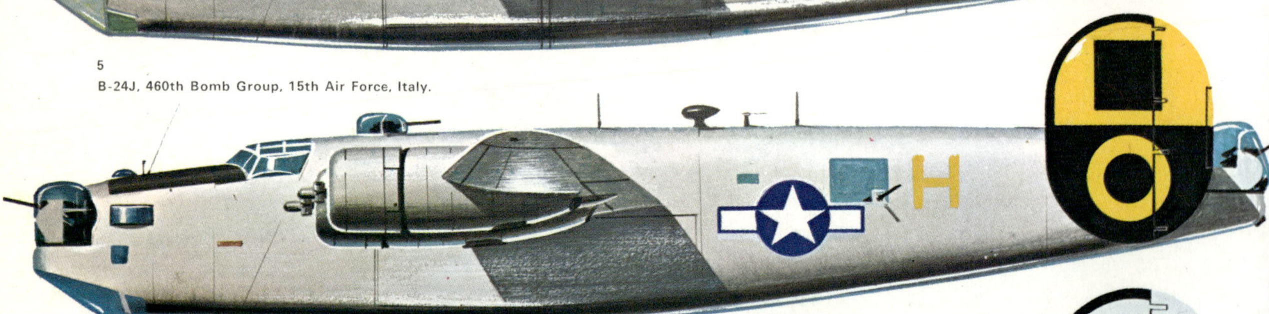


6

B-24J, 465th Bomb Group, 15th Air Force, Italy.

© WARD

1
B-24D, 376th Bomb Group, 512th Squadron, 9th Air Force, Western Desert. 'Strawberry Bitch'.

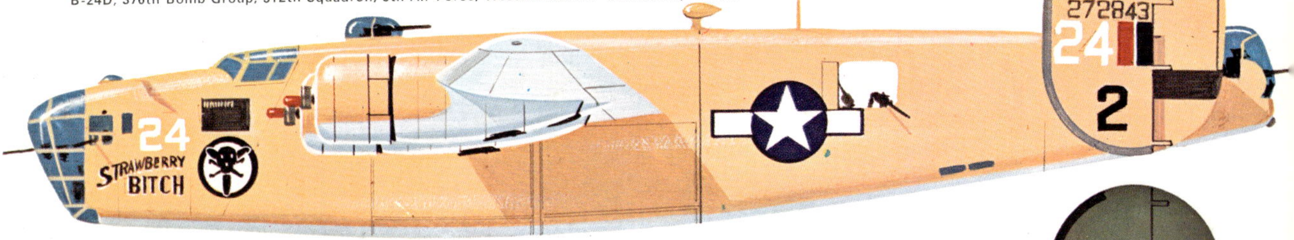


2
B-24D, 28th Bomb Group, 11th Air Force, Aleutians.

3
B-24D, in Sea-search camouflage.

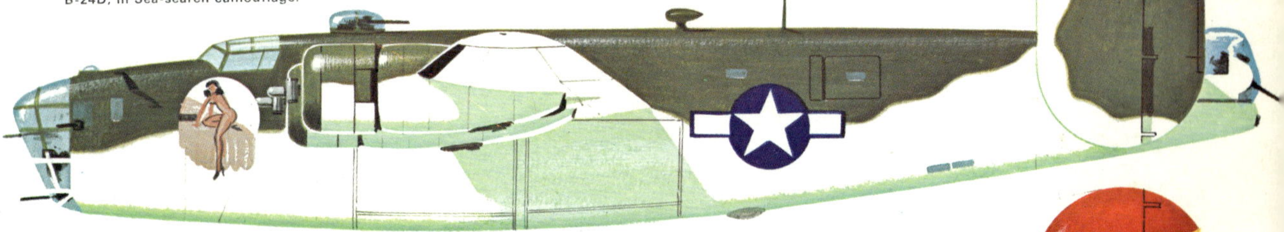


4
B-24M, All Weather Flying Center.

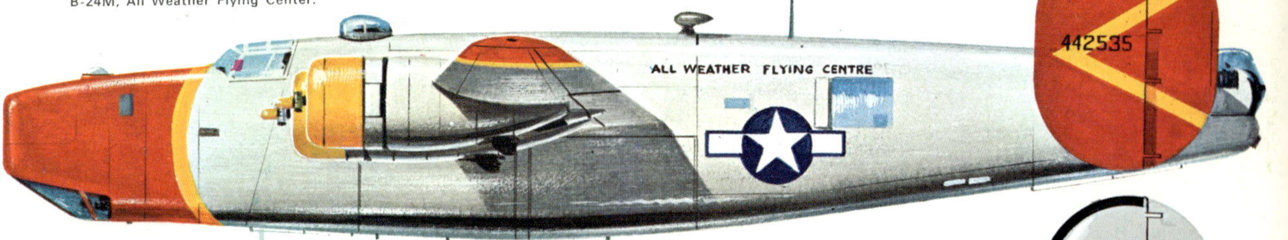


5
C-109, IXth Troop Carrier Command, ETO.

6
EZB-24, Aero Icing Research Laboratory.

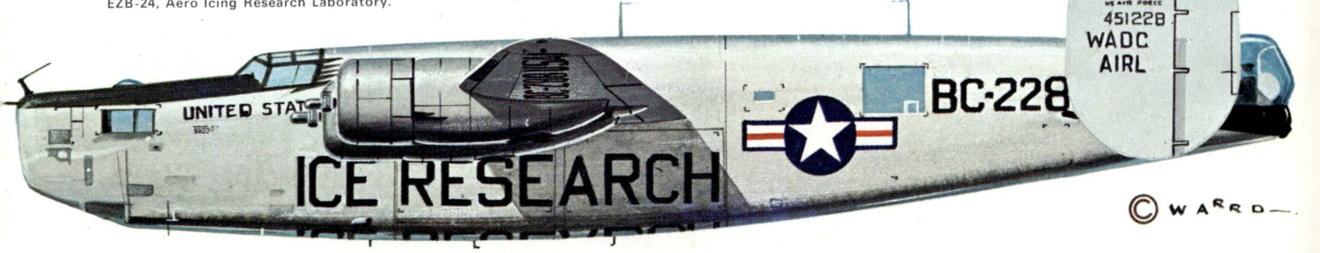

F

1

B.VI, No. 356 Squadron, RAF, SEAC.

2

B.VI, No. 99 'Madras Presidency' Squadron, RAF, SEAC.

3

B.VII, No. 355 Squadron, RAF, SEAC.

4

B.VI, No. 104 Squadron, RAF, SEAC.

5

B.VI, No. 223 Bomber Support Squadron, 100 Group, RAF.

6

B.VI, No. 5 Operational Training Unit, RAF, Boundary Bay, Abbotsford, British Columbia, Canada.

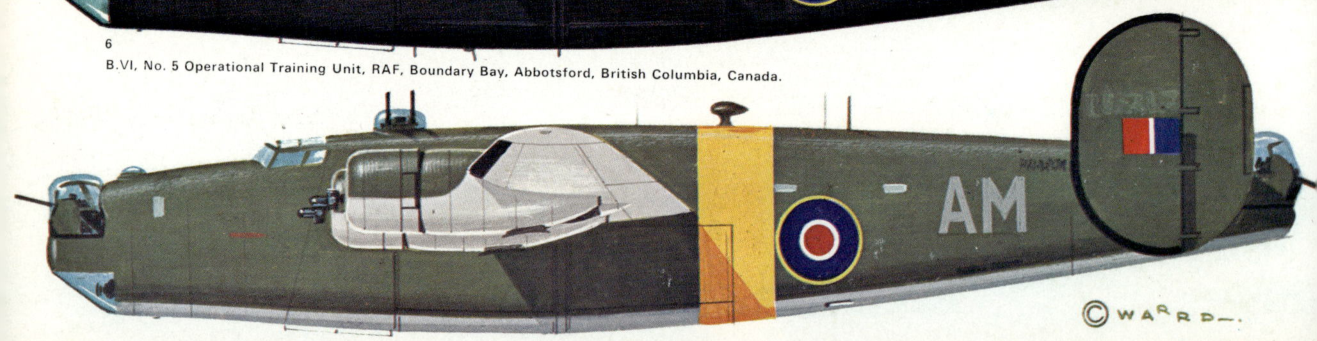

1
GR.III, No. 120 Squadron, Coastal Command, RAF.

2
GR.VI, Coastal Command, RAF, SEAC.

3
GR.VI, No. 311 'Czechoslovakian' Squadron, Coastal Command, RAF.

4
GR.VI, No. 220 Squadron, Coastal Command, RAF.

5
C.VIII, No. 53 Squadron, RAF.

6
B.VIII, No. 86 Squadron, RAF.

1
GR.VI 311th Squadron, Czechoslovakian Air Force.

2
GR.VI, No. 321 Squadron, Koninklijke Marine, Netherlands East Indies.

3
B-24J, No. 201 Flight, Royal Australian Air Force.

4
B-24J, No. 24 Squadron, Royal Australian Air Force.

5
B-24M, Chinese Nationalist Air Force.

6
B-24J, Indian Air Force.

Above: Nose art gone mad! A B-24J of the 43rd Bomb Group, 5th Air Force, SWPA. (Peter M. Bowers).

Above: B-24J of the 43rd Bomb Group, 5th Air Force, flying along the New Guinea coast. (USAF).

Above: One of a formation of B-24J's of the 494th Bomb Group, 7th Air Force, under attack by Japanese fighters over Kolono Bay during raid on Celebes, NEI. 8th Janaury 1944. (USAF).

Below: Overall black B-24J of the 11th Bomb Group, 7th Air Force, Rio Negros strip. (Frank F. Smith).

Above: B-24D of the 7th Bomb Group, 10th Air Force, India, on the run in to the target area, the dockside warehouses at Rangoon. (USAF).

Above: B-24D of the 7th Bomb Group, 10th Air Force, returning to its dispersal area at Pandaveswar Field after a mission. (USAF).

Left: B-24J of the 7th Bomb Group, 10th Air Force, coming in to land at Kurmitola Field, India, Janaury 1944. (USAF).

Left: B-24J of the 7th Bomb Group attacking the Bilin railroad bridge in Burma, 13th November 1944. (IWM).

Below: The last B-24 Liberator to be built, so the caption says. 10th Air Force, India. (USAF).

Above: A pair of B-24J's of the 308th Bomb Group, 14th Air Force, CBI, heading out for targets in Hunan Province, China. (USAF).

Below: B-24J of the 308th Bomb Group, 375th Squadron, landing on a Chinese airfield, 14th Air Force, CBI. (R. M. Bueschel).

Below: Interesting Liberator of an unknown unit on a Chinese airfield. (R. M. Bueschel).

Below: B-24L of an unknown unit flying over the 'Hump' enroute for Kunming, China. 14th Air Force, CBI. (USAF).

Above: B-24D probably of the 28th Bomb Group, 11th Air Force, Aleutians. (IWM).

Above: Radar equipped B-24D of the 28th Bomb Group, 11th Air Force, flying past a snow streaked Aleutian volcano. (USAF).

Below: 28th Bomb Group B-24D forced landed on the cliffs due to its home base being fog bound. (USAF).

Below: 'Boogow', a B-24D of the 28th Bomb Group, 11th Air Force warming up on Elmendorf Field, Alaska, note 100lb bombs on sled. (USAF).

Above: B-24D in Sea-search scheme. (Peter M. Bowers).

Above: C-109 tanker (converted B-24J) taking off from Myitkyina, Burma. (USAF).

Below: Chinese reinforcements for Gen. Stilwell boarding a C-87 at Yunnanyi airfield in China for the Burma front. (USAF).

Below: C-109 of the IXth Troop Carrier Command, ETO. (USAF).

Below: EZB-24 of the Aero Icing Research Laboratory. (Peter M. Bowers).

Above: B-24J of No. 21 Squadron, RAAF. Serial A72–56. (Frank F. Smith).

Right: B-24J of No. 23 Squadron, RAAF. (Frank F. Smith).

Left, two pictures & below: B-24J's of No. 24 Squadron, Royal Australian Air Force. GR–P serial unknown, GR–D serial A72–34, GR– serial A72–170. Chevrons on fin and rudder are 'Wing Man' not squadron markings.
(photos Frank F. Smith).

Above: B-24J of No. 201 Flight, Royal Australian Air Force. Serial A72–186. (Frank F. Smith).

Left: B-24J of No. 12 Aircraft Repair Depot, RAAF. Serial A72–185. (Frank F. Smith).

Below: Nice flying shot of a B-24J of No. 7 OTU, Tucumwal, New South Wales. (Frank F. Smith).

Above: A72–41 a B-24J of No. 7 OTU. Yellow 41 outlined black. (Frank F. Smith).

Below: Line-up of No. 7 OTU B-24J's at Tucumwal, NSW. (IWM).

Above: B.VI of No. 5 OTU, Boundary Bay, Abbotsford, British Columbia, 1944/45. (J. E. H. Fail).

Above: Line-up of No. 5 OTU B.VI's, note yellow fuselage band. (J. E. H. Fail).

Above: OD B.VI of No. 40 Squadron, RAF, Foggia, Italy April 1945. BL–Q, KH–328. (Frank F. Smith).

Below: B.VI in standard RAF night bomber scheme, No. 40 Squadron, Foggia, Italy, April 1945. BL–V, KL–574. (Frank F. Smith).

Above: B.VI of No. 356 Squadron, RAF, leaving the target area after attack on Japanese Headquarters at Kyaukse south of Mandalay, Burma. Note SNAKE above D ahead of serial KH272. (IWM).

Below: Liberators of No. 356 Squadron leaving Ramree Island, south of Akyab on the Arakan coast after bombing Japanese installations. (IWM).

Above: A pair of Liberators of No. 99 Squadron 'Madras Presidency' Squadron, RAF, attacking a Japanese target in Burma. Note Squadron marking on rudder, a small white disc. (IWM).

Above: B.VI of No. 355 Squadron, RAF, heading back to base after attack on Japanese target. Note black and white stripes on rudder, OD camouflage. (IWM).

Below: B.VIII of No. 215 Squadron taking off from an Indian airfield. Squadron marking two horizontal white stripes on rudder. (RAAF).

GR.III of No. 120 Squadron, Coastal Command, RAF. (IWM)

Line-up of GR.III's of No. 120 Squadron at Aldergrove, Northern Ireland. (IWM).

Above: GR.VI of No. 220 Squadron in standard Coastal Command scheme. (IWM).
Below: Line-up of GR.VI's of No. 220 Squadron, Coastal Command, at Lagens, Azores. (IWM).

Above: GR.VI of the 311th Squadron, Czechoslovakian Air Force, Prague airfield 1945–6. Ex No. 311 Squadron, Coastal Command, RAF. (Zdenek Titz).

Above: Line-up of Liberators of No. 321 Squadron, Koninklijke Marine, Netherlands East Indies. (G. H. Kamphuis).

Above & below: B-24M of the Chinese Nationalist Air Force. (photos, above Dave Lucabaugh via R. M. Bueschel, below via Earl Reinert).

Below: B-24J of the Indian Air Force. (USAF).

Above: PB4Y–1 Privateer returning to a UK base from patrol over the Bay of Biscay. White and grey camouflage with red surround to the National insignia.(USMC).

Above: PB4Y–1 on Munda, New Georgia, Solomon Islands, late 1945. (Earl Reinert).

Above: Overall yellow PB4Y–1 from the Naval Aircraft Modification Unit, Johnsville, PA. (Peter M. Bowers).
Below: PB4Y–2 in sea-blue/grey and white scheme, unit unknown. (Peter M. Bowers).

Above: PB4Y–2, unit unknown, note armament details. (Peter M. Bowers).

Below: Nice flying shot of a grey/white Privateer, note extent of white under surfaces. (USMC).

Below: Grey/white PB4Y–2 of an unknown unit, note radar under nose. (Earl Reinert).

NATC based PB4Y–2 with all armament removed. (Peter M. Bowers).

Above: Line-up of PB4Y–2's of Escadrille 28F, Aeronavale. (ECA via Jean Cuny).

Below: PB4Y–2 of Escadrille 8F prior to re-numbering 28F in mid-1953. (ECA via Jean Cuny).

Below: PB4Y–2 Privateer of the Chinese Nationalist Air Force. (USAF).

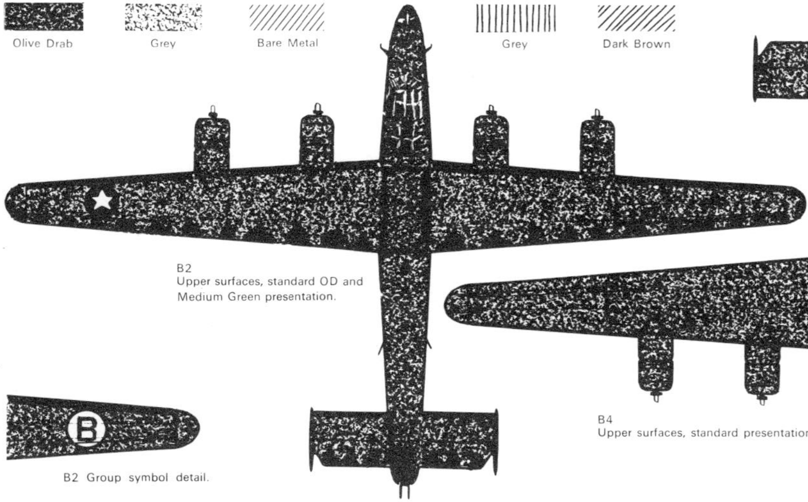

B2
Upper surfaces, standard OD and Medium Green presentation.

B2 Group symbol detail.

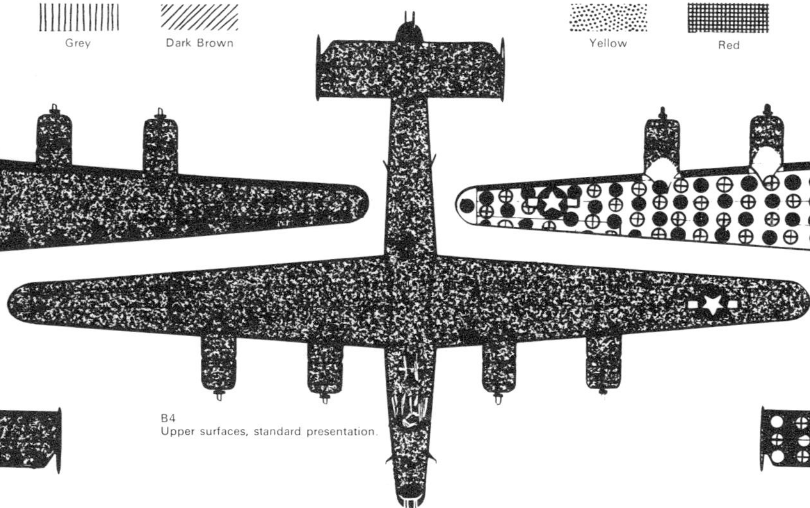

B4
Upper surfaces, standard presentation.

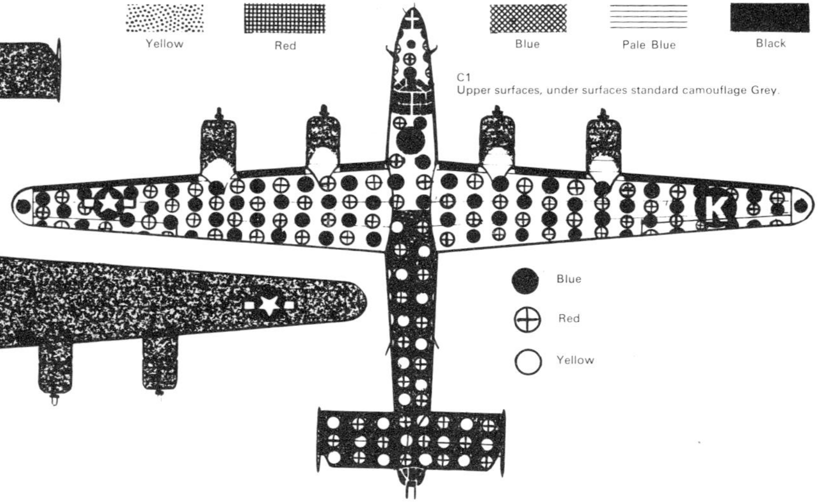


C1
Upper surfaces, under surfaces standard camouflage Grey.

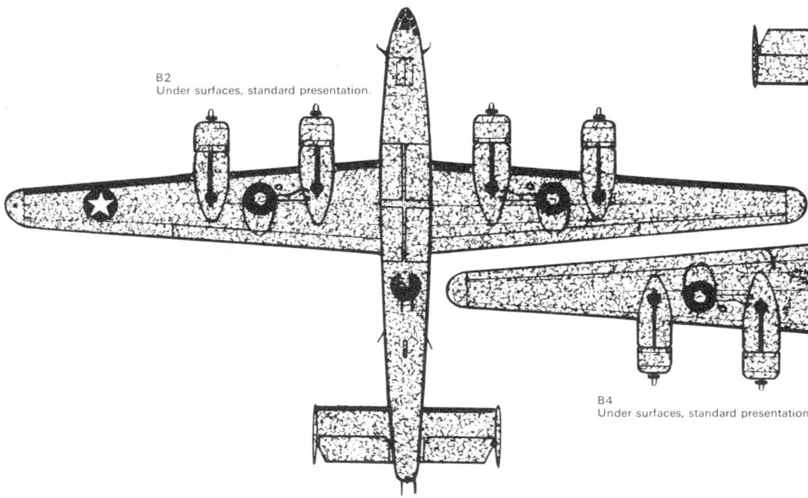

B2
Under surfaces, standard presentation.

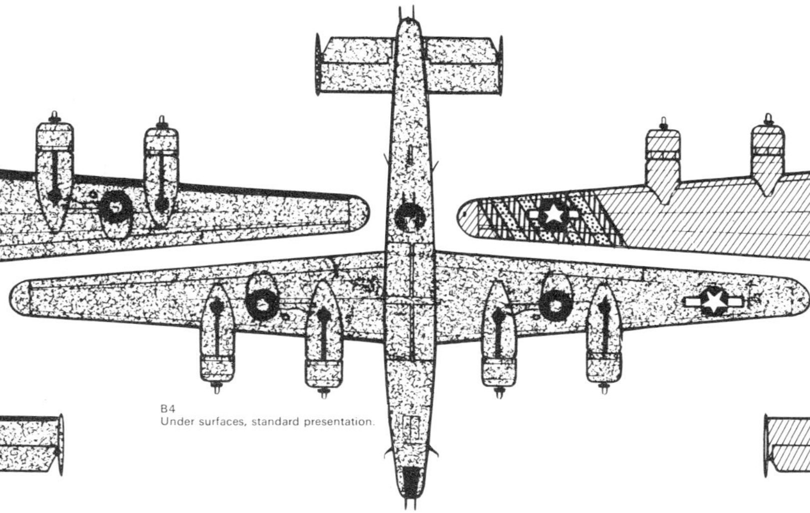

B4
Under surfaces, standard presentation.

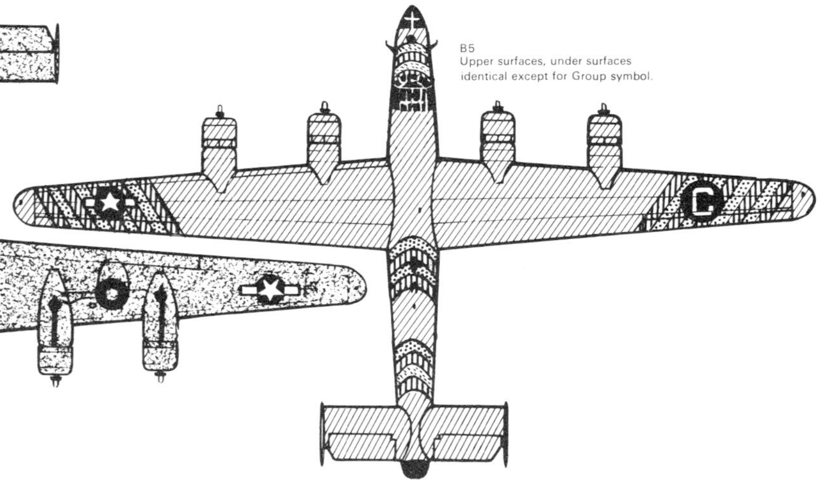

B5
Upper surfaces, under surfaces identical except for Group symbol.

D1
Upper surface detail, under surfaces identical except no red on tail-plane.

D5
Tail-plane detail.

F6
Upper surface detail, under surfaces pale grey, note yellow fuselage band.

F1
Upper surface detail, SEAC roundels, under surfaces pale grey.

A4
Upper and under surfaces identical.

F3
Upper and under surfaces identical.

F5
Upper surface detail, under surfaces black overall.